The moon and the stars may fall to the earth,
The earth with all its mountains and dwelling places may disappear,
And space itself may disappear,
But it is impossible for Buddha to tell a lie.

Meeting the Buddhas

Our Closest Friends and Helpers

THARPA PUBLICATIONS

USA · UK · CANADA

AUSTRALIA · HONG KONG

Published 2010

Tharpa Publications
47 Sweeney Road
Glen Spey, New York 12737
USA
www.tharpa.com

Tharpa Publications
Conishead Priory
Ulverston, Cumbria
LA12 9QQ, England
www.tharpa.com

Tharpa Publications has offices around the world, and our books are
available in most major languages.

Painting of Amitayus on p. 18 (and details from it on pp. 18–19) by
Sherab Thubten. Paintings by Chating Jamyang Lama on pp. 4 (Buddha
Shakyamuni), 8–9 (Offering Goddesses, detail of a Je Tsongkhapa thangka),
9 (Avalokiteshvara), 10–11 (Je Tsongkhapa and Sons, including details
in page background), 15 (Manjushri), 16–17 (background images, detail
of a Refuge Assembly thangka), 21 (White Tara), 22 (Medicine Buddha),
24 (Vajrasattva), and 30–31 (clouds, detail of a Je Tsongkhapa thangka).

Prayer verses and mantras are taken from sadhanas (prayer booklets)
published by Tharpa Publications.

Library of Congress Control Number: 2009930541

Hardback ISBN-13 978-0-9817277-4-5 (ISBN-10 0-9817277-4-3)

Set in Arno Pro by Tharpa Publications USA

Printed in the United States of America on acid-free paper.

*Profits received by Tharpa Publications from
the sale of this book will be donated to the*
NKT-IKBU International Temples Project
*A Nonprofit Buddhist Organization,
Building for World Peace*
www.KadampaTemples.org

Contents

Acknowledgement

This book has arisen from the compassionate vision and actions of the Spiritual Teacher, Venerable Geshe Kelsang Gyatso. Through his great kindness we have the opportunity to meet the Buddhas, listen to Buddha's teachings that offer us real protection from suffering and problems, and find pure spiritual friends who will travel with us on a path to world peace. May everyone have this precious opportunity.

Meeting the Buddhas

Our Closest Friends and Helpers

Liberating Prayer ~ Praise to Buddha Shakyamuni

O Blessed One, Shakyamuni Buddha,
Precious treasury of compassion,
Bestower of supreme inner peace,

You, who love all beings without exception,
Are the source of happiness and goodness;
And you guide us to the liberating path.

Your body is a wishfulfilling jewel,
Your speech is supreme, purifying nectar,
And your mind is refuge for all living beings.

With folded hands I turn to you,
Supreme unchanging friend,
I request from the depths of my heart:

Please give me the light of your wisdom
To dispel the darkness of my mind
And to heal my mental continuum.

Please nourish me with your goodness,
That I in turn may nourish all beings
With an unceasing banquet of delight.

Through your compassionate intention,
Your blessings and virtuous deeds,
And my strong wish to rely upon you,

May all suffering quickly cease
And all happiness and joy be fulfilled;
And may holy Dharma flourish for evermore.

Who is Buddha?

Buddha means "Awakened One," someone who has awakened from the sleep of ignorance and sees the truth perfectly. Many people have become Buddhas in the past, and we all have the potential to become a Buddha in the future.

There is nothing Buddhas do not know, because they have developed perfect wisdom. Buddhas also have perfect love and compassion. Their love embraces every human, animal, insect, and all other living beings, and they care for each one equally.

For this reason, the Buddhas are our closest friends and helpers. Benefitting every living being is their main purpose, so the Buddhas are always beside us, working to lead us to happiness. If we remember this with faith and request their help, they can easily teach, bless, guide, and protect us. Then one day we will be able to benefit others in the same way!

The Three Jewels of Buddhism

A Buddhist is someone who turns to the Three Jewels of Buddha, Dharma, and Sangha for help to solve his or her daily problems.

Buddha Shakyamuni gave 84,000 teachings during his life. By practicing these teachings, called Dharma, we learn to protect ourselves from problems and difficulties.

The spiritual friends who follow Buddha's advice are called Sangha. They encourage us, assist us with our Dharma practice, and set a good example for us to see and follow.

We can think that the Three Jewels work together like this: Buddha is a supreme doctor who knows how to cure our sickness, Dharma is the medicine that has the power to make us well, and Sangha are the nurses who help us take this medicine.

How lucky we are to have the Three Jewels!

I and all sentient beings, until we achieve enlightenment,
Go for refuge to Buddha, Dharma, and Sangha.

Buddha Shakyamuni

In northern India* in 624 BC a baby was born to Queen Mayadevi and King Shuddhodana. They called the little boy Siddhartha. The King wanted his son to be a ruler like him, so he kept him very busy in the palace. Prince Siddhartha was kind to everyone, and learned perfectly every subject he studied. When he was grown, he married Yasodhara and had a son.

One day during a visit to the city, Siddhartha saw so much pain and suffering. He passed people who were very old and sick. He saw a human corpse, and finally he saw a monk. The prince wanted desperately to discover how to end suffering for everyone, and begged to leave the palace to try. He said goodbye to his family and began a long, difficult journey.

After training his mind for six years, Siddhartha knew he was very close to his goal. He walked to a place now called Bodh Gaya, sat under a Bodhi tree, and promised not to rise from meditation until he became a Buddha. Many frightening and tempting maras surrounded Siddhartha and tried to stop him. Because of the strength of Siddhartha's concentration on love, however, even Devaputra, King of Demons, could not succeed. Although he and his armies threw many terrible weapons at Siddhartha, these turned into flowers and fell to the ground.

As the sun rose, Siddhartha's mind transformed into that of a Conqueror Buddha with immense power to help all living beings. Forty-nine days later, he began to teach others how to follow the path to pure happiness.

OM MUNI MUNI MAHA MUNIYE SÖHA

*now Nepal

5

Green Tara is a female Buddha. Her name means "Rescuer." She is swift as the wind, and rescues living beings from the fears and dangers of this world. There are 21 different Taras in the Pure Land of Potala, all coming from the heart of Green Tara, with excellent powers such as curing diseases, stopping fighting, and ending bad dreams. We can easily recognize Green Tara because she sits with her right foot forward, ready to instantly rise when we call her.

We can think that Green Tara is our Buddha Mother and feel very close to her. Tara can appear as anyone and anything, and she is always in our life—watching over us, guiding us, and giving us what we need. Whenever we find ourselves in a difficult situation, all we need to do is to stop worrying and ask Mother Tara for her help. With the great love of a Buddha Mother, Green Tara will quickly solve our problems.

OM TARE TUTTARE TURE SÖHA

Green Tara

One day, Avalokiteshvara, the Buddha of Compassion, looked out at all the suffering in the world and he began to weep—so much help was needed. His tears formed a deep pool, and a beautiful lotus sprang up in its center. The lotus opened and Green Tara was born. "Please do not cry! I will help you free living beings from sorrow," Tara said.

Homage to Tara, the Swift One, the Heroine,
Whose eyes are like a flash of lightning,
Who arose from the opening of a lotus,
Born from the tears of the Protector of the
    Three Worlds.

Avalokiteshvara

The Buddha who appears to teach us how to increase our love and compassion is named Avalokiteshvara. Compassion is a powerful wish in our heart to stop forever all the different types of pain that people, animals, and others experience within their bodies and minds.

Avalokiteshvara has a body that is clear white in color, and he shines with rainbow light. He sits on a white lotus seat with a moon at his back. His legs are crossed in the vajra position, and his beloved Spiritual Guide, Buddha Amitabha, is always with him on his crown. Smiling gently at all living beings with eyes of love, Avalokiteshvara wears silk clothing and sparkling necklaces, anklets, and bracelets.

OM MANI PÄME HUM

Avalokiteshvara usually appears with four arms. Two of his hands are pressed together at his heart, holding a wishfulfilling jewel. His second left hand holds a white lotus flower and his second right hand holds a crystal mala. These objects remind us that Avalokiteshvara is a completely pure being who can lead us all to a blissful world where there is no suffering, only happiness.

If we want to help those we love be free from pain and problems, we can pray to Avalokiteshvara. With his blessings, their suffering will be removed and our own love and compassion will also increase. Then one day we too will become a Buddha of Compassion.

With your compassionate nectar please purify swiftly
The karma and delusion we have accumulated since beginningless time.
And with your hands of compassion please swiftly lead me
And all living beings to the Pure Land of Bliss.

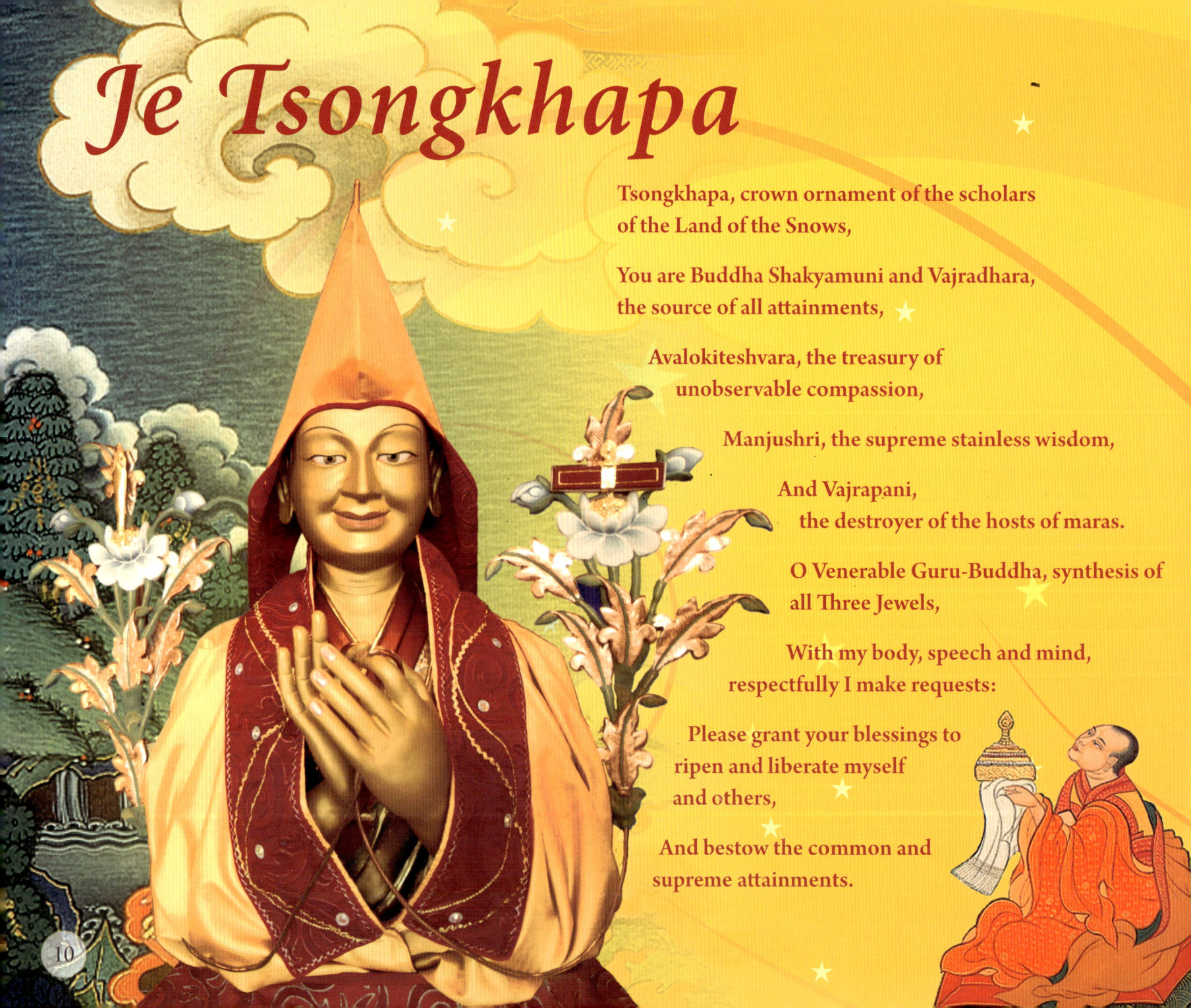

Je Tsongkhapa

Tsongkhapa, crown ornament of the scholars
of the Land of the Snows,

You are Buddha Shakyamuni and Vajradhara,
the source of all attainments,

Avalokiteshvara, the treasury of
unobservable compassion,

Manjushri, the supreme stainless wisdom,

And Vajrapani,
the destroyer of the hosts of maras.

O Venerable Guru-Buddha, synthesis of
all Three Jewels,

With my body, speech and mind,
respectfully I make requests:

Please grant your blessings to
ripen and liberate myself
and others,

And bestow the common and
supreme attainments.

Je Tsongkhapa lived in Tibet, the Land of the Snows, from 1357 to 1419. When he was born, special signs showed he was Buddha Manjushri appearing in the world again. Later, people understood that he held in his heart the wisdom, compassion, and spiritual power of all the Buddhas. He became a famous teacher. Guru Tsongkhapa had miracle powers, but he never used them in public or acted high or special. He was always seen to be humble, showing a perfect example of a Buddhist monk, and giving pure and clear Dharma teachings to help everyone.

Guru Tsongkhapa was like a mother patiently teaching her children step by step everything they need to know. In this way, he showed thousands of people how to become a Buddha in one lifetime.

When Je Tsongkhapa passed away, the whole country grieved. Because they could no longer see him, many artists made statues and paintings of him, and some of these did amazing things—speaking, smiling, disappearing, rising into space, and even stopping a war! It is said that if we keep a statue of Je Tsongkhapa in our home, we will never be poor and we will easily gain wisdom.

Through Je Tsongkhapa's kindness we have Buddha, Dharma, and Sangha in our life today. There is no one kinder than our Guru, Je Tsongkhapa!

OM AH GURU VAJRADHARA SUMATI KIRTI SIDDHI HUM

OM VAJRA WIKI WITRANA SÖHA

E veryone needs a best friend, helper, and protector. Today people have a special close connection with Dorje Shugden, and he is all of these! Just as a rainbow appears from the sky, Dorje Shugden appears from the wisdom of Buddha Manjushri.

One of Dorje Shugden's main jobs is to help us increase our wisdom and compassion, keeping these "jewels" safely in our hearts. Another is to make sure we always have the chance to practice Buddha's teachings so that we can be happy and free from pain and problems.

Dorje Shugden looks a little different than most of the Buddhas in this book. He rides a white snow lion and may show a fierce, wrathful face to scare off anything that would hurt us. Because he loves us and cherishes our spiritual practice, he protects us like a father would. His yellow robes tell us he has taken a vow as a monk never to harm, always to help. His golden hat and sword show his wisdom. The heart he holds symbolizes his compassion. On his arm sits a mongoose that spits jewels—this reminds us that Dorje Shugden arranges perfect conditions for us to improve our spiritual practice.

In the New Kadampa Tradition of Mahayana Buddhism, we pray to Je Tsongkhapa and Dorje Shugden every day to request blessings, help, and protection from these two holy beings. We love these special prayers. They are called *Heart Jewel*.

Dorje Shugden

Before me in the center of red and black fire and wind,
On a lotus and sun, trampling demons and obstructors,
Is a terrifying lion, which is powerful and alert.
Upon this sits the great king Dorje Shugden,
The supreme Heart Jewel of Dharma Protectors.
His body is clothed in the garments of a monk,
And on his head he wears a round, yellow hat.
His hands hold a sword and a heart of compassion.
To his followers he shows an expression of delight,
But to subdue demons and obstructors he displays
    a wrathful manner.

13

The roar of your speech, like the sound of thunder,
rouses us from the sleep of the delusions.

Manjushri is the Wisdom Buddha. He became a Buddha long before the time of Buddha Shakyamuni. Manjushri appears most often with an orange colored body, which shines like the sun. Above his head he holds a flaming wisdom sword, reminding us that he cuts through the darkness in our mind that is the root of all pain and problems. His fingers hold the stem of an upala flower, which blooms near his ear. At the center of the flower is a special Dharma text, *The Perfection of Wisdom Sutra.*

What is wisdom? It is not the same as being smart or clever. For example, some people use the science they have learned in school to make weapons, and cats are very clever when it comes to catching mice. But these are not examples of wisdom. Wisdom never causes harm to ourselves or others; it only brings happiness. When we have wisdom, we do not feel confused or unhappy. Our mind is peaceful and we understand things clearly and easily. With eyes of wisdom, we will always know what is best to do.

Manjushri

There once was a king named Ajatashatru who had strong faith in Manjushri. One day he invited Manjushri to a banquet at his home, and after the meal he rose to offer Manjushri an exquisite cloak. Just as he was presenting the cloak, however, Manjushri disappeared.

"Who is Manjushri? Where is Manjushri?" the king wondered. By thinking like this, he came very close to understanding the truth about the way things really are.

Since Manjushri had vanished, the king decided to try on the cloak. As he put it around his shoulders, he asked the same questions about himself. "Who am I? Where am I? Who is the king? Where is the king?"

Unable to find a real, truly existent king as he contemplated these questions and meditated on them, he quickly realized emptiness directly and became a Superior Being on the Path of Seeing!

OM AH RA PA TSA NA DHI

Vajrapani is the Buddha of spiritual power. Sometimes Vajrapani appears in a dark blue wrathful form, and other times he appears as a Bodhisattva—a person who is not yet a Buddha but never forgets that he or she wants to become one to liberate all living beings from suffering.

Once, a large group of close students came to Buddha Shakyamuni to receive a teaching. Bodhisattva Vajrapani was among them. Buddha turned to Bodhisattva Vajrapani and said, "This is the time to show your power."

Hearing these words, Bodhisattva Vajrapani displayed to the crowd the thunderbolt vajra he held in his right hand. Then he placed it on the ground. "Is there anyone here who has the power to pick up this vajra?" Buddha asked.

Bodhisattva Manjushri, the most powerful among them, tried with all his strength and found he could not. Turning to Buddha in surprise, he said, "I cannot move the vajra. Why is this?"

Buddha replied, "This shows the great power of Bodhisattva Vajrapani. He has the power to destroy the real enemy of living beings—the inner poison of the delusions."

If we pray to Vajrapani, he will help us destroy our own anger, craving, and confusion.

VAJRAPANI

May all suffering quickly cease
And all happiness and joy be fulfilled.

OM AH VAJRAPANI
HUM HUM PHAT

17

There is nothing more precious to us than our life. We might think wealth and beautiful things are important and work very hard to get them, but we already have our most precious possession. Using our life in meaningful ways, we have the opportunity to experience every happiness, including a Buddha's enlightenment! Understanding this, we want to live a long time to enjoy ourselves and to practice Dharma.

Amitayus is the Buddha of long life, good fortune, and wisdom. He appears as a red-colored Buddha with a peaceful, smiling face, holding a vase full to the brim with long-life nectar. On top of the vase is a wish-granting tree. His beautiful body is decorated with shining earrings, throat ornaments, bracelets, anklets, pearls, and very long necklaces. He sits on a peacock throne and is surrounded by a mass of brilliant light.

If we are facing sickness or dangers that may take our life, we can turn and make sincere prayers to Buddha Amitayus. He has the power to protect us, and his blessings can increase our wisdom and help us live a long time.

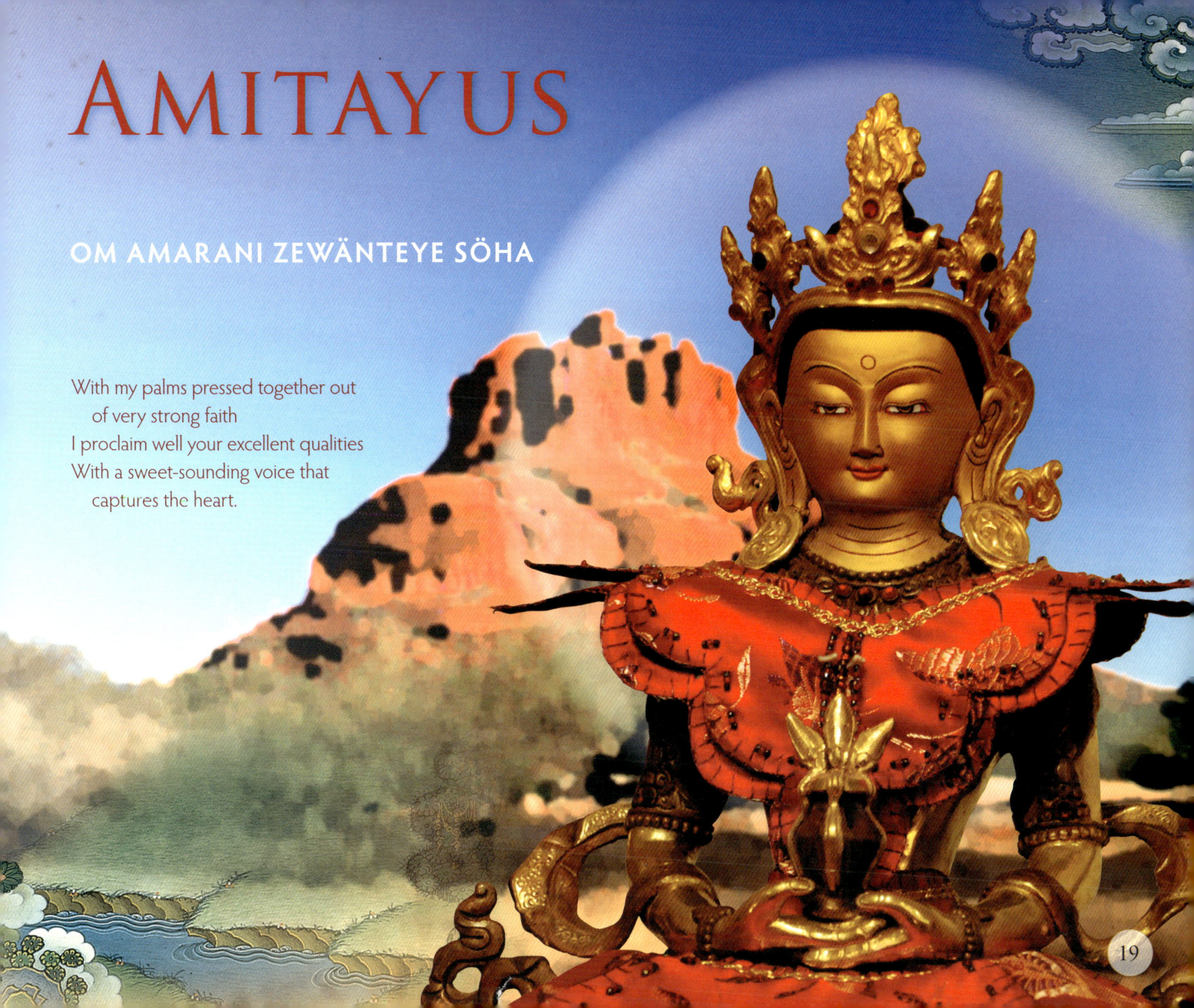

AMITAYUS

OM AMARANI ZEWÄNTEYE SÖHA

With my palms pressed together out
   of very strong faith
I proclaim well your excellent qualities
With a sweet-sounding voice that
   captures the heart.

WHITE TARA

OM TARE TUTTARE TURE
MAMA AYUR PUNAYE GYANA
PUTRIM KURU YE SÖHA

White Tara is a female Buddha who increases the lifespan, wisdom, and good fortune of living beings. If we pray to her with faith, she has special abilities to protect us from contagious diseases, and the dangers of fire, floods, earthquakes, and other disasters. White Tara's blessings are immensely powerful—they can even destroy the terrible Lord of Death who arrives to steal away our life!

White Tara has a white-colored body made of wisdom light. She has seven eyes—two on her face, plus one on her forehead, and each hand and foot. Wearing exquisite garments, she sits on a white lotus in the vajra position. She rests her right hand on her knee with her palm open in the gesture of supreme giving. With her left hand, she holds an upala flower.

White Tara is the kind and compassionate Buddha Mother of all living beings. And just like Green Tara, we receive White Tara's help as swiftly as the wind moves.

When I see the signs of untimely death,
May I immediately receive the blessings of Arya Tara.

21

Medicine Buddha

Because our world is filled with diseases, problems, and dangers that arise from wild minds and hurtful actions, our strong prayers to heal ourselves and others are very important.

The Buddha Doctor whose blessings can free us from inner and outer sicknesses is called Medicine Buddha. When we invite him, he appears from Lapis Jewel Land with a blue-colored body. He wears a monk's robes and holds an arura flower—a special medicine plant—and a jeweled bowl filled with medicine nectar.

If we have faith in him, he has the power to cure heavy, painful diseases of our body and mind, protect us from many dangers, and free us forever from the three poisons.

When we visualize him to make prayers, Medicine Buddha sits above the crown of our head and his beautiful name is Buddha Medicine Guru, Great King with the Radiance of a Lapis Jewel. He is joined by six more Medicine Buddhas sitting in the vajra position, one above the other. Next comes King of Clear Knowing, who is red. Above him is Melodious Ocean of Dharma Proclaimed, with a pink body. Above him is Supreme Glory Free from Sorrow, who is also pink. Next is Stainless

Excellent Gold, above him is King of Melodious Sound, and above him is Glorious Renown of Excellent Signs, all who have golden bodies.

We make abundant offerings to these Buddhas, request their help and protection, and then receive their healing blessings. Reciting Medicine Buddha prayers, we can also gain a special power of body, speech, and mind to perform healing actions to benefit others.

TAYATHA OM BEKHADZE BEKHADZE MAHA BEKHADZE BEKHADZE RANDZAYA SAMUGATE SÖHA

May the frightened be released from their fears,
May those in captivity be freed,
May the powerless be endowed with power,
And may people think only of benefiting one another.

23

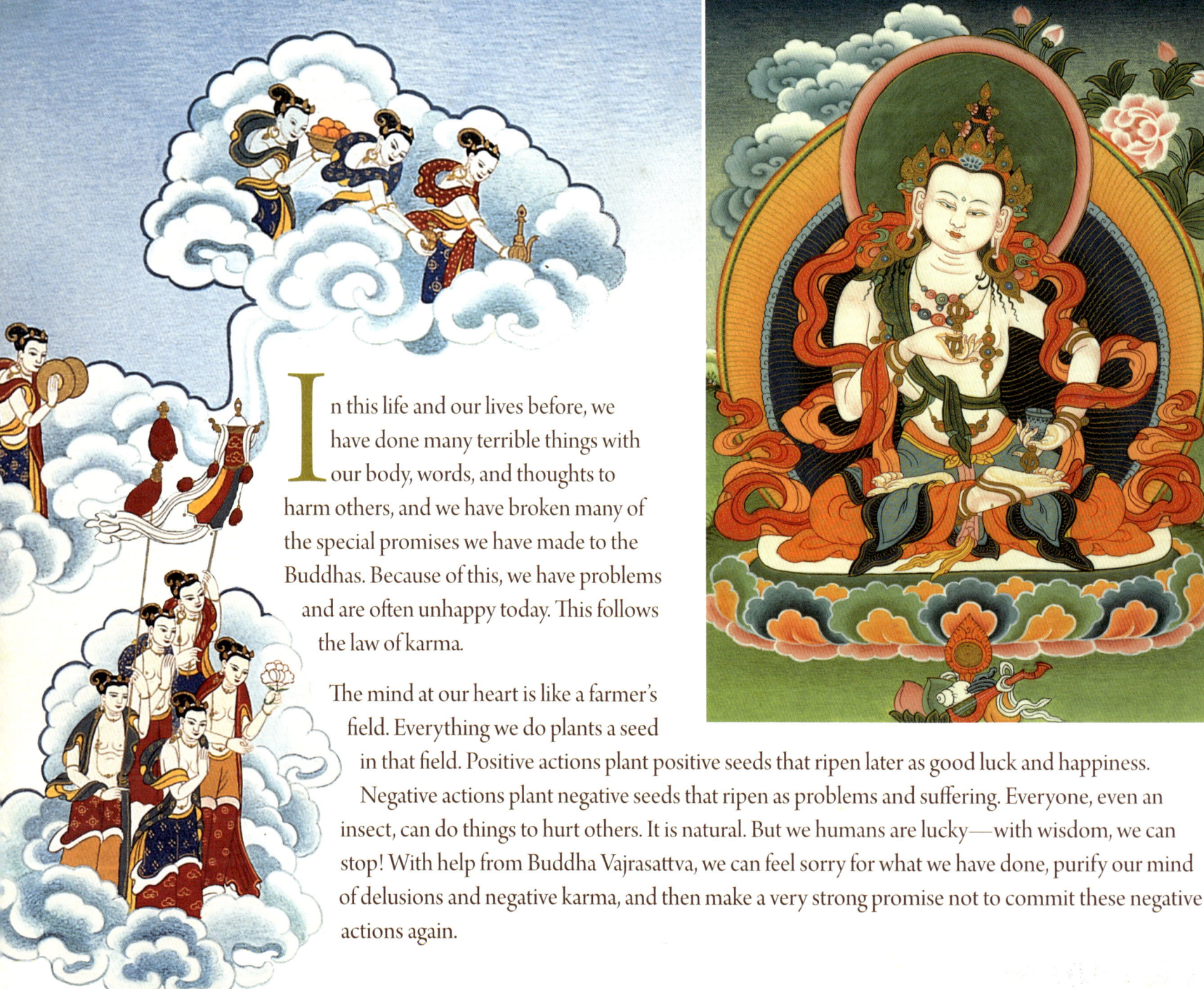

In this life and our lives before, we have done many terrible things with our body, words, and thoughts to harm others, and we have broken many of the special promises we have made to the Buddhas. Because of this, we have problems and are often unhappy today. This follows the law of karma.

The mind at our heart is like a farmer's field. Everything we do plants a seed in that field. Positive actions plant positive seeds that ripen later as good luck and happiness. Negative actions plant negative seeds that ripen as problems and suffering. Everyone, even an insect, can do things to hurt others. It is natural. But we humans are lucky—with wisdom, we can stop! With help from Buddha Vajrasattva, we can feel sorry for what we have done, purify our mind of delusions and negative karma, and then make a very strong promise not to commit these negative actions again.

Vajrasattva

OM VAJRA
SATTÖ SARWA
SIDDHI HUM

Vajrasattva has
a white-colored
body, and he holds a
vajra near his heart and
a bell below it. He wears
colorful silk garments, ribbons,
and sparkling jewelry. When we
visualize him and request his help
by reciting his mantra, he comes to the
crown of our head and blesses our mind
with streams of cleansing wisdom nectar.

Out of unknowing and confusion
I have transgressed and broken
    my commitments.
O Guru Protector, please protect me.

The Great Mother Prajnaparamita appears inside the heart of Buddha Shakyamuni to teach us about the perfect wisdom of all the Buddhas. She helps faithful practitioners in two ways: to defeat maras—inner and outer obstructing demons—and to find perfect lasting peace and joy through meditating on emptiness.

Prajnaparamita has a body made of golden wisdom light. Her four arms show us that she has arisen from the wisdom of all the Buddhas of the four directions. Her first right hand holds a golden nine-pronged vajra, her left hand holds the *Perfection of Wisdom Sutras*, and Prajnaparamita's remaining two hands rest together in her lap to remind us of the importance of training in meditation. She wears glittering jewels and colorful garments of the softest silk.

Just looking at Prajnaparamita teaches us about emptiness. Her lovely form appears to our mind like a rainbow, a mirage, or a dream. Buddha said, "A magician creates various things such as horses, elephants, and so forth; his creations do not actually exist. You should know all things in the same way." Prajnaparamita guides us to the truth about the way things really exist, opening our wisdom eyes!

OM AH PRAJNAPARAMITA HUM HUM PHAT

Prajnaparamita

Form is empty; emptiness is form.

**TAYATHA OM GATE
GATE PARAGATE
PARASAMGATE
BODHI SÖHA**

O Blessed One Shakyamuni Buddha,
Great Mother Prajnaparamita,
And all Buddhas of the ten directions,
To you I prostrate, make offerings
  and go for refuge.

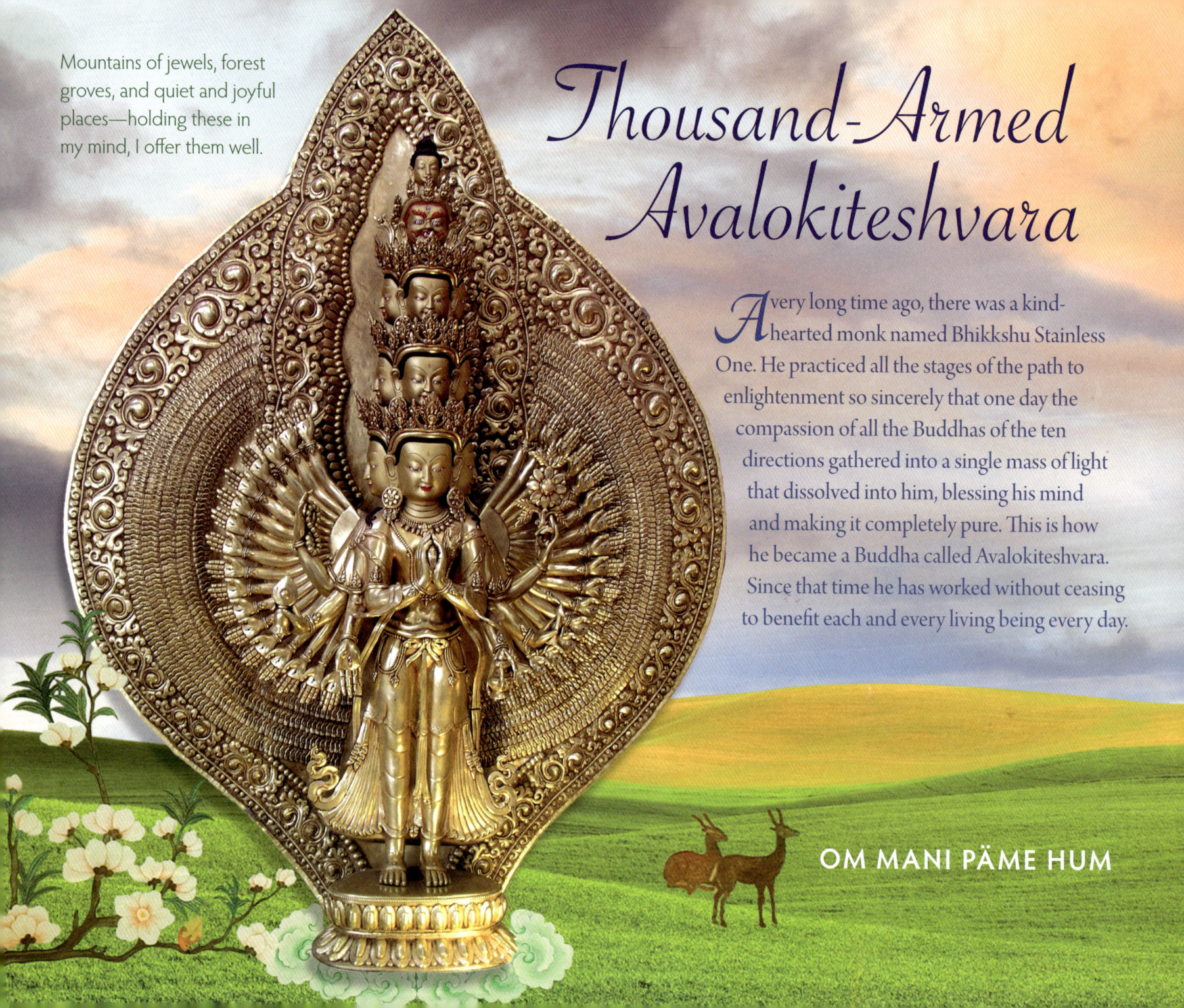

Mountains of jewels, forest groves, and quiet and joyful places—holding these in my mind, I offer them well.

Thousand-Armed Avalokiteshvara

A very long time ago, there was a kind-hearted monk named Bhikkshu Stainless One. He practiced all the stages of the path to enlightenment so sincerely that one day the compassion of all the Buddhas of the ten directions gathered into a single mass of light that dissolved into him, blessing his mind and making it completely pure. This is how he became a Buddha called Avalokiteshvara. Since that time he has worked without ceasing to benefit each and every living being every day.

OM MANI PÄME HUM

From his Pure Land of Sukhavati, Thousand-armed Avalokiteshvara, Buddha of Compassion, arises to help us develop peaceful, happy minds, control our delusions, solve our problems, and finally become an enlightened being like him.

In this special form, Avalokiteshvara's many arms remind us that the thousand Buddhas of this Fortunate Aeon are all within his heart. He shows eleven faces, including his top face, which is the face of his beloved Guru, Buddha Amitabha. His ten lower faces teach us that he works endlessly to help suffering living beings throughout the world with countless emanations, which include pure spiritual teachers.

Avalokiteshvara is standing, his first two hands pressed together at his heart. Six more hands hold a crystal mala, a lotus, a long-necked vase, a wheel, and a bow and arrow. The rest of his 992 hands are all in the mudra of supreme giving, with an eye in each palm to see where help is needed.

Thousand-armed Avalokiteshvara wants most of all to release all living beings from suffering. Making strong prayers to him, we can continually receive his powerful blessings for ourselves and others!

The loving-kindness of all the Buddhas appears in the form of Maitreya. He is known as the Protector of the hundreds of Deities of the Joyful Land, which is also named Tushita Pure Land. He has a golden-colored body, a stupa at his crown, and two hands in the mudra of turning the Wheel of Dharma. He holds flowers that support a wheel and a long-necked vase. Maitreya often sits with his feet on the ground, showing that he is ready to descend from his Pure Land. He will do this in the future as the Fifth Buddha.

What would it be like to live in Tushita Pure Land? Beings there do not suffer or have problems. They do not become old, sick, or die. All good things come easily. There is no hunger or thirst, no fighting or dangers. Precious mountains, wishfulfilling trees, clear lakes, and pools are everywhere. In the trees, many birds that have come from Maitreya's heart sing the meaning of Dharma. Gardens filled with jewels and heavenly flowers surround bathing pools in which young gods and goddesses play. The whole ground is made of jewels, and is so completely pure and smooth that touching it brings great joy. In the center is Yiga Chodzin Palace, where Buddha Maitreya lives with thousands of Bodhisattvas.

Many great Buddhist Teachers chose to go to Tushita Pure Land when they passed away, including Je Tsongkhapa. From this heaven, they appear today in different forms to help us. When we invite Je Tsongkhapa, he descends immediately from Maitreya's heart on a thread of compassion-clouds. If we remember this and keep Je Tsongkhapa close, then when we die our mind will follow the thread to Tushita Pure Land, too.

Maitreya

Asanga wanted very much to see Buddha Maitreya directly, so he found a mountain cave and began to meditate. During his retreat, however, he sometimes felt alone and discouraged. After 12 years, he finally quit. Leaving the mountain, he came across an old dog lying on the path. She was dying, and her body was covered with maggots. Asanga's heart was filled with compassion for all suffering beings. As he began to gently remove the maggots, the dog suddenly transformed into Maitreya. Asanga was shocked. "Why did I need to wait such a long time to see you?" he asked. Maitreya explained he had been with Asanga since the start of his retreat, but Asanga had not been able to see him because his mind was not yet pure. It was Asanga's compassion that finally purified his mind so his wish could be fulfilled.

Especially through my meditation on
   the three aspects of love
May I always care for all living beings
   without exception.

OM MOHI MOHI MAHA MOHI SÖHA

Vajradhara

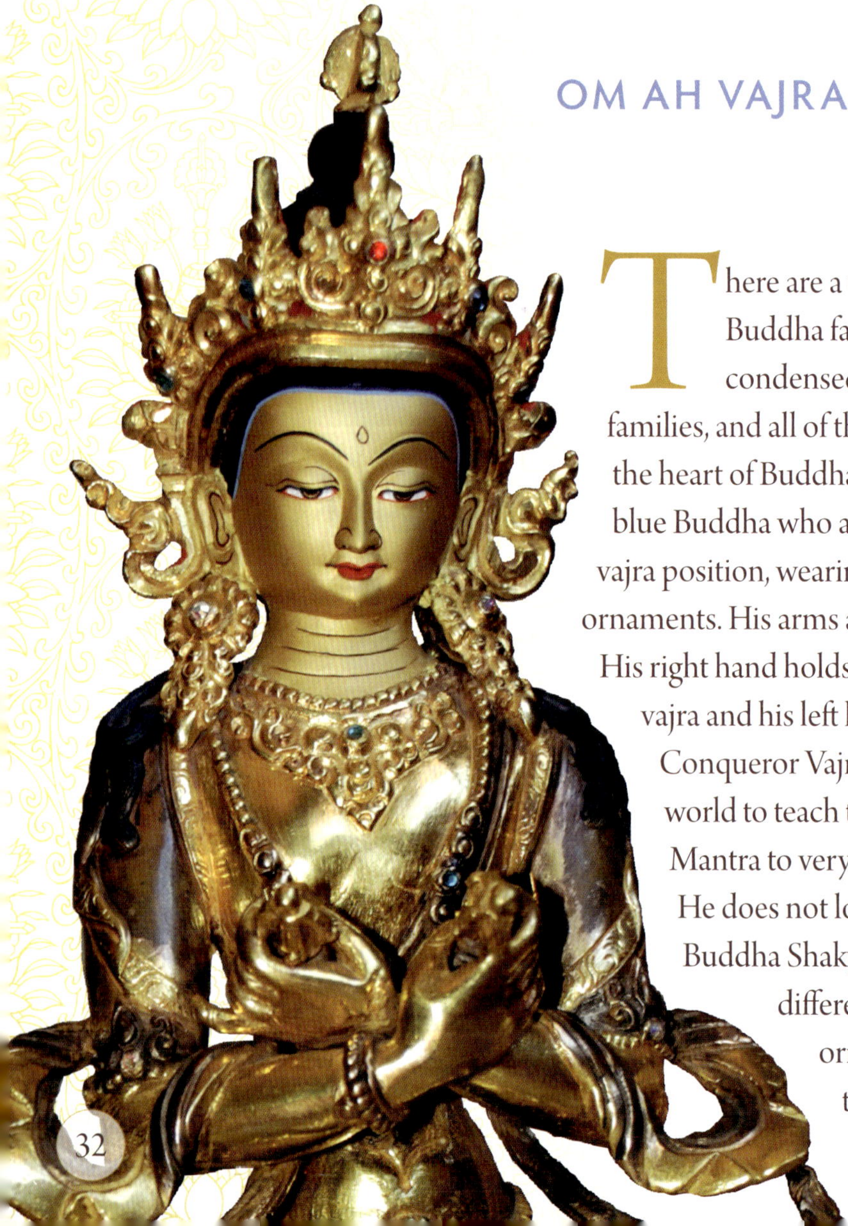

OM AH VAJRADHARA HUM

There are a total of one hundred Buddha families. These can all be condensed into the five Buddha families, and all of these are held within the heart of Buddha Vajradhara. He is a blue Buddha who appears sitting in the vajra position, wearing glittering jeweled ornaments. His arms are crossed at his chest. His right hand holds a golden, five-pronged vajra and his left hand holds a silver bell. Conqueror Vajradhara appeared in this world to teach the quick path of Secret Mantra to very fortunate practitioners. He does not look very much like Buddha Shakyamuni, having a different color, shape, and ornaments, but he is really the same being.

The family of Buddha Akshobya

The family of Buddha Vairochana

The family of Buddha Ratnasambhava

The family of Buddha Amitabha

The family of Buddha Amoghasiddhi

Now that we have met the Buddhas . . .

We Can Visualize a Living Buddha

One of the best methods to receive the Buddhas' blessings and increase our faith is to gaze at an image of a Buddha again and again, regarding it as an actual Buddha. When we see an image of Buddha, for instance, like one of the paintings or photographs in this book, instead of thinking of it as just a drawing or picture, we can try to feel we are in the presence of a real, living Buddha and consider his kindness in caring for us and all living beings. We remember that Buddha is our best friend, guide, and protector. He smiles gently and looks at us with eyes of love, like a father would. Thinking like this and feeling very close, we can ask Buddha for anything.

We can pray to Buddha for ourselves, our family, our friends, people we don't know, and animals. We can recite the special prayers that have been written in printed prayer booklets, called sadhanas, or we can use our own words. Our prayers can be short or long, silent, sung, or spoken. The words might be beautiful, like poetry, or we can have a simple conversation with Buddha in our heart: "Please Buddha, care for me always. Teach and guide me. Protect me from danger. Bless me so I can better help others. Help me to become just like you."

We Can Know that Buddhas Are Everywhere

Buddhas are everywhere; there is no place where Buddhas do not exist. With strong faith, wherever we are, we can imagine and believe that living Buddha Shakyamuni is before us, surrounded by all the Buddhas and Bodhisattvas, like the full moon surrounded by the stars.

Visualizing Buddhas wherever we are is not make-believe. It is a way of opening our mind to what is already there. It is our ignorance that clouds our mind and prevents us from seeing holy beings directly. On a rainy day, although we cannot see the sun we have no trouble imagining it shining behind the clouds because we know it is there. In the same way, if we imagine the Buddhas are in front of us, our mind will make a strong connection with them and over time we will know them well and see them very clearly.

We Can Think, "What Will It Be Like When I Am a Buddha?"

When I am enlightened, I will be completely free from all faults, all sufferings, and every kind of pain and problem, and I will have every good quality. I will have great power—perfect ability to help other living beings—and my mind will be a source of peace and happiness for all of them! As many living beings as there are, I will have as many emanations. Just as one moon shining in the sky appears in every lake and water in the world, when I am a Buddha my emanations will cover and protect everyone.

How wonderful to be a Buddha with the power to give happiness to all living beings everywhere. We can feel so inspired imagining this. One day, it will be true!

Praying For World Peace

Prayers for World Peace

By working to develop peace in our own hearts, we are taking the most important step toward creating peace in our world. Without inner peace, world peace is impossible. This means if we wish for a peaceful world to appear, we must all take responsibility to improve our good hearts, to benefit others more, and to stop harming them and ourselves with our bodies, words, and thoughts. Deciding to give others happiness is a very powerful action. If we remove inner poisons such as anger from our hearts, and cultivate love and peace there instead, we will easily solve our problems and improve our love, compassion, and wisdom. In this way world peace will naturally appear!

Venerable Geshe-la's Instructions

"Our job is to pray for world peace—anytime, anywhere. With compassion, we make dedications and pray to develop and maintain inner and outer peace and harmony. We know right now there are so many dangers, so many problems, wars, and terrible things—so we try to repair them, to pacify them, to cause all these dangers and obstacles to cease. We pray that the people of this world will experience peaceful, happy minds and meaningful lives. And through our pure intention, our good works, the power of these prayers, and particularly through receiving the blessings of enlightened beings, these results will definitely come. Our job is to pray."

—*given at the opening of the US Kadampa World Peace Temple, October 2006*

KADAMPA TEMPLES DEDICATED TO WORLD PEACE

US Kadampa World Peace Temple at Kadampa Meditation Center (KMC) New York

Manjushri KMC (UK)

KMC France

KMC Brazil

KMC Germany

KMC Australia

Kadampa Buddhist Temples take many forms. Some are custom-built according to a special design developed by Geshe Kelsang Gyatso based on traditional Buddhist architecture. Others are adapted from existing buildings in, or near, some of the world's major cities. Others are included within Hotel Kadampas. Many more Temples are planned for the future. Whatever form they take, Kadampa Temples bring great benefit to everyone who sees or enters them. Through their doorways we find the path to lasting peace and happiness!

Glossary

Blessing ～ The transformation of our mind from negative to positive, unhappy to happy, and weak to strong with help from the holy beings.

Bodhichitta ～ The "mind of enlightenment." A mind that wishes to become a Buddha to free all living beings from suffering.

Bodhisattva ～ A person who has bodhichitta continuously, but who has not yet become a Buddha.

Compassion ～ A positive, peaceful mind that wishes others to be free from suffering.

Delusions ～ Bad mental habits (or inner poisons) that make our mind unpeaceful, unhappy, and out of control. There are three main delusions: anger, craving, and confusion, and others that come from these, such as jealousy, pride, and doubt.

Dharma ～ Buddha's teachings and the inner qualities that come from practicing them. Dharma means "protection." By practicing Buddha's teachings we protect ourself from problems and suffering.

Emanation ～ Buddhas' minds can appear in any form at all to help living beings. These forms are called emanations.

Emptiness ～ The things we normally see do not exist the way they appear. Emptiness is the truth about the way things really are.

Enlightenment ～ A Buddha's mind.

Faith ～ This is a naturally positive mind that sees good qualities in pure or holy objects.

Geshe ～ This title, which means "virtuous friend," is given by Kadampa monasteries to excellent Buddhist students.

Guru ～ Spiritual Guide or Teacher.

Karma ～ The actions of our body, speech, and mind, and the effects of these actions. The effect of positive actions is happiness, and the effect of negative actions is suffering.

Love ～ A mind wishing others to be happy. There are three types of love: affectionate love, cherishing love, and wishing love.

Mantra ～ A special prayer said in Sanskrit. Reciting a mantra is a method to request a Buddha to appear so we can receive his blessings, help, and protection. (All the Buddhas' mantras are in capital letters in this book.)

Maras ～ Demons and any negative forces that hold us back from enlightenment, such as delusions or an early death.

Meditation ～ A mind that focuses on virtue and is the main cause of inner peace and happiness.

Merit ～ The good luck or good fortune that comes from good deeds. It has the power to increase our positive qualities and bring happiness.

Mudra ～ Hand gestures.

Refuge ～ Actual protection. To go for refuge to Buddha, Dharma and Sangha means to have faith in them and to turn to them for protection from all fears and suffering.

Sangha ～ The community of sincere Buddhist friends who help us on our spiritual path.

Stupa ～ A tower-like object that is a representation of Buddha's mind.

Three Jewels ～ Buddha, Dharma, and Sangha. They are called "jewels" because they are both rare and precious.

Three poisons ～ The three main delusions of anger, craving, and confusion. See also "Delusions."

Vajra ～ "Indestructible like a diamond and powerful like a thunderbolt." This is also the name given to a metal ritual object.

Vajra position (or Vajra posture) ～ A cross-legged seated position in which the feet rest soles upward on the thighs, and hands rest together in the lap. This is a perfect posture for meditation.

Wisdom ～ Virtuous intelligence that makes us and others happy.

Wrathful ～ A controlled, positive action or appearance that is strong and fierce, coming from a mind of love and a wish to benefit, without any anger.

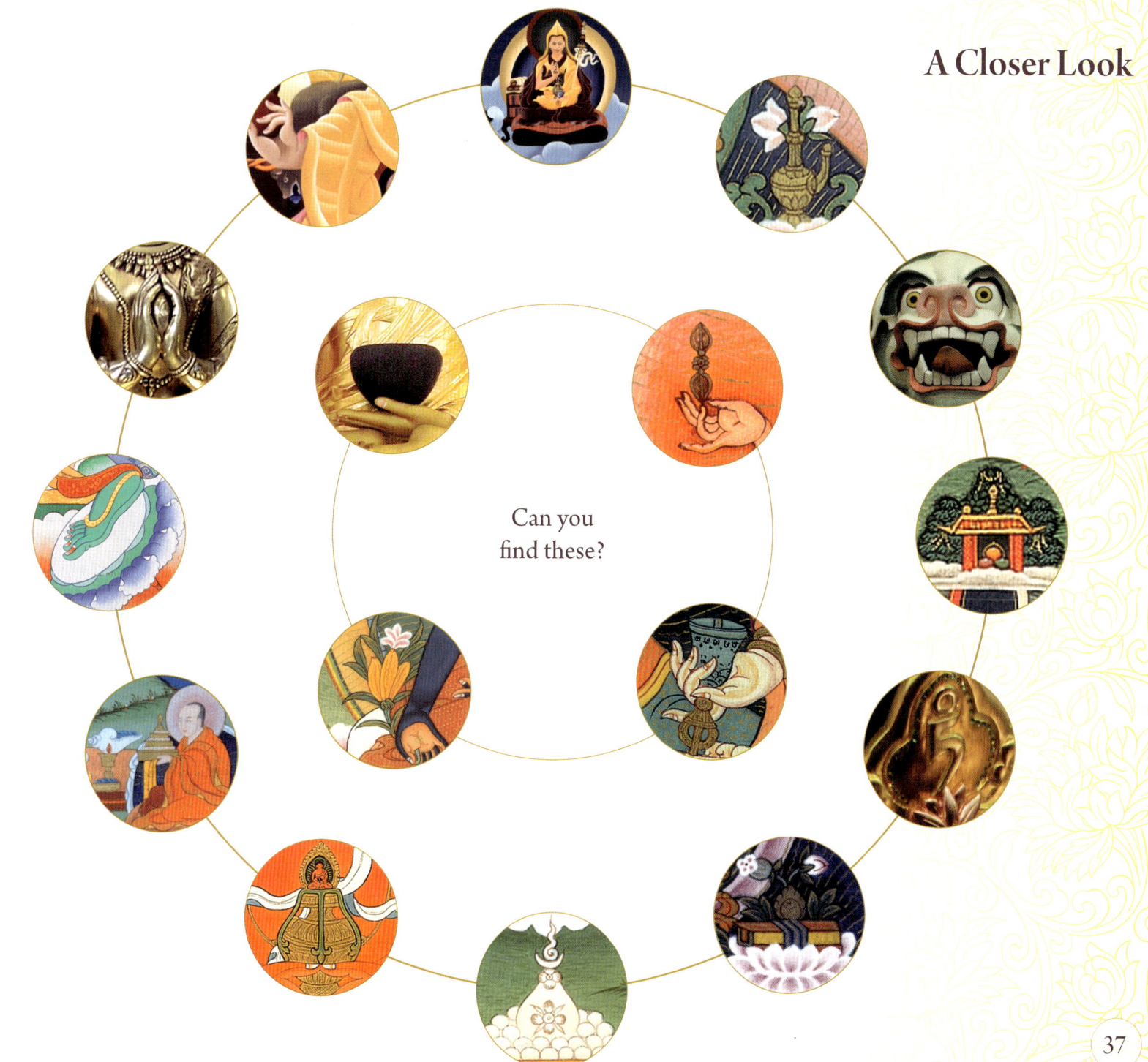

Can you
find these?

Learn More About . . .

Modern Kadampa Buddhism

The New Kadampa Tradition–International Kadampa Buddhist Union (NKT-IKBU) is a Mahayana Buddhist Tradition that was founded by Venerable Geshe Kelsang Gyatso in the lineage of the famous Buddhist meditators and scholars Atisha (AD 982–1054) and Je Tsongkhapa (AD 1357–1419). It is an international non-profit company registered in England, and an independent Buddhist tradition that has no political affiliations.

For more information and a directory of NKT-IKBU Dharma Centers worldwide, please see www.Kadampa.org.

Tharpa Publications

Tharpa Publications is the international publishing company of the NKT-IKBU and the exclusive publisher of Venerable Geshe Kelsang Gyatso's books. Tharpa also produces a wide range of audio books, meditation and prayer CDs, prayer booklets, and Buddhist art, which are all available at www.Tharpa.com, in leading bookstores, and at NKT-IKBU Centers.

All profits from the sale of Tharpa books and products are donated to the International Temples Project (ITP) and are used to build Kadampa Temples around the world.

International Temples Project

The ITP was established by Venerable Geshe Kelsang Gyatso with a vision to build a Kadampa Buddhist Temple dedicated to inner and outer peace in every major city in the world. To learn more about current ITP projects, visit www.KadampaTemples.org.

Venerable Geshe Kelsang Gyatso

Venerable Geshe Kelsang Gyatso is a fully accomplished meditation master, renowned Buddhist teacher, and author. At the age of eight, he entered a monastery in Tibet where he was ordained as a Buddhist monk. He spent almost 40 years in study and meditation before moving to England in 1977. Venerable Geshe-la, as he is affectionately called by his students, has made his life's work sharing Buddha's teachings in order to help his students transform their minds and lives, and fulfill their potential.

Venerable Geshe-la has written 20 books on Buddhism that clearly explain how to solve our human problems by following the path to enlightenment. Through his compassionate efforts, NKT-IKBU Buddhist teachers are now helping and guiding students at over 1100 locations in more than 40 countries.

Dedication

All of the virtues we have collected in compiling this book with a wish to benefit to others, we now dedicate to world peace.

We pray that all hatred and harming stops in this world, that there is a definite end to quarrelling, fighting, and all acts of violence and war.

We pray that what is dangerous will be pacified, what has been damaged will be repaired, and whatever is hurting anyone will cease.

We pray for the well-being of those we love, and for those we may not yet love. May everyone be happy, and may they never be separated from their happiness.

With compassion for people, animals, and all living beings, we pray to cherish one another perfectly.

May everyone find the opportunity to lead a happy and meaningful life.

May all suffering quickly cease
And all happiness and joy be fulfilled;
And may holy Dharma flourish for evermore.

NKT - IKBU